Cambridge **C2 Proficiency**

C2 Key Word Transformation

200 exam-styled practice exercises

Jane Turner

PROSPERITY EDUCATION
www.prosperityeducation.net

Registered offices: Sherlock Close, Cambridge
CB3 0HP, United Kingdom

© Prosperity Education Ltd. 2023

First published 2023

ISBN: 978-1-913825-73-7

This publication is in copyright. Subject to statutory exception and to the provisions of relevant collective licensing agreements, no reproduction of any part may take place without the written permission of Prosperity Education.

'Use of English', 'Cambridge C2 Proficiency' and 'CPE' are brands belonging to The Chancellor, Masters and Scholars of the University of Cambridge and are not associated with Prosperity Education or its products.

The moral rights of the author have been asserted.

For further information and resources, visit:
www.prosperityeducation.net

To infinity and beyond

Contents

Introduction	iv
Test 1	1
Test 2	5
Test 3	9
Test 4	13
Test 5	17
Test 6	21
Test 7	25
Test 8	29
Test 9	33
Test 10	37
Test 11	41
Test 12	45
Test 13	49
Test 14	53
Test 15	57
Test 16	61
Test 17	65
Test 18	69
Test 19	73
Test 20	77
Answers	81

Introduction

Welcome to this edition of sample tests for the Cambridge C2 Proficiency, Part 4: Key Word Transformation, designed specifically for students preparing for the challenging Use of English section of the (CPE) examination, but also suitable for any English language student working at CEFR C2 level.

C2 results are given against the *Cambridge English Scale*, which is the average score for the four skills and the Use of English section of the test. In order to allow ample time for the reading parts (Parts 5–7) of Paper 1, it is advisable that candidates complete The Use of English section (Parts 1–4) as quickly as possible while maintaining accuracy.

This resource contains 200 exam-styled, single-sentence assessments, each carrying a lexical/lexico-grammatical focus, testing lexis, grammar and vocabulary. Each assessment comprises a sentence, followed by a 'key' word and an alternative sentence conveying the same meaning as the first but with a gap in the middle. Use the key word provided to complete the second sentence so that it has a similar meaning to the first sentence. You cannot change the keyword provided. Each correct answer is broken down into two marks. Next to each sentence transformation answer you will find a guide indicating the focus of the two parts of the answer: either G (grammatical) or L (lexical). At this level, grammar and lexis are often integrated but this device gives a rough indication to help you with your revision for the exam.

Author **Jane Turner** is an associate lecturer in EAP/EFL at Anglia Ruskin University, Cambridge, and an EFL materials writer for international exam boards, universities and publishers. She previously worked as a Cambridge ESOL examiner for the British Council, and holds an MA in Educational Management and Cambridge CELTA and DELTA.

Visit www.prosperityeducation.net for more C2 Proficiency exam practice.

Cambridge C2 Proficiency

Use of English

Part 4

Test 1

Cambridge C2 Proficiency Use of English
Part 4 — Key word transformation — Test 1

For questions 1–10, complete the second sentence, using the word given, so that it has a similar meaning to the first sentence. Do not change the word provided and use between three and eight words in total. In the separate answer sheet, write your answers in capital letters, using one box per letter.

1 Most of Ben's colleagues were quite surprised when he decided to quit.

   SOMETHING

   Ben's resignation _____ to his team.

2 Helen said many nice things to Rob about his work in the feedback meeting.

   PAY

   Helen made sure to _____ during their discussion.

3 In my opinion, the point Carla raised in the discussion was irrelevant.

   FAILED

   I _____ Carla's point.

4 The minister's anger could be understood, despite the carefully worded statement.

   LINES

   When you _____, it was possible to detect the minister's anger.

5   Passing the proposed law would be an important step for workers' rights.

    BE

    If it _____, this law would surely improve workers' rights.

6   I'm going to trust Pat, even if her explanation doesn't make much sense.

    DOUBT

    I'm prepared to give _____ however unlikely her story is.

7   Let's talk to Ben before we make any rash decisions about what happened.

    JUMP

    It is important _____ before we hear from Ben.

8   Voters remain unconvinced about the merits of the council's proposal.

    YET

    The council _____ is worth supporting.

9   The manager was not willing to ignore such serious allegations by Maria.

    ALLEGED

    What Maria _____ be disregarded by the manager.

10 The price increases you described are also happening in our country.

    BOAT

    We _____ you in terms of rising prices.

Answer sheet: Key word transformation Test No.

Name _____ Date _____

Write your answers in capital letters, using one box per letter.

1.
2.
3.
4.
5.
6.
7.
8.
9.
10.

Cambridge C2 Proficiency Use of English

Part 4

Test 2

Cambridge C2 Proficiency Use of English

Part 4 — Key word transformation — **Test 2**

For questions 1–10, complete the second sentence, using the word given, so that it has a similar meaning to the first sentence. Do not change the word provided and use between three and eight words in total. In the separate answer sheet, write your answers in capital letters, using one box per letter.

1 We noticed that no professional coaches were helping their clients online.

GAP

We identified _____ online sports coaching.

2 Gaining more professional opportunities is something I really want.

LONG

I _____ professional horizons.

3 The panel regarded Ben's credentials as being unsuitable for the role.

DEEMED

Ben's qualifications _____ suitable for the job.

4 None of her colleagues regretted their behaviour.

SINGLE

Not a _____ remorse for their actions.

5 If you want to get fitter, nothing is more effective than training consistently.

ROUTE

Consistency is the most _____ improved fitness.

6 The minister had to face many embarrassing questions in the press conference.

SUBJECTED

The media _____ of awkward questions.

7 The preference of staff is for remote working over coming to the office.

SOONER

Our employees _____ home than commute.

8 Let's not forget just how much Katya knows about IT.

WEALTH

Katya _____ which should not be overlooked.

9 The problem stems from her letting employees do whatever they wanted.

FOOT

If _____ her staff, we would not be in this mess.

10 Louise came up with the term 'brand master'.

COINED

It _____ 'brand master'.

Answer sheet: Key word transformation Test No. ☐

Name _____   Date _____

Write your answers in capital letters, using one box per letter.

1.
2.
3.
4.
5.
6.
7.
8.
9.
10.

Cambridge C2 Proficiency

Use of English

Part 4

Test 3

Cambridge C2 Proficiency Use of English

Part 4   Key word transformation   **Test 3**

For questions 1–10, complete the second sentence, using the word given, so that it has a similar meaning to the first sentence. Do not change the word provided and use between three and eight words in total. In the separate answer sheet, write your answers in capital letters, using one box per letter.

1. It isn't unusual for Carla to sulk when things aren't going the way she wants.

    PRONE

    Carla _____ when she doesn't get her own way.

2. You will have to stay alert when you work with children.

    KEEP

    Working with children will _____ toes.

3. There are limits to the number of times we can excuse Jon's rude behaviour.

    ONLY

    There are _____ make excuses for Jon.

4. Their constant complaints ruined the whole trip for me.

    COMPLAINING

    I didn't enjoy the trip because _____ everything.

5 Peter has fallen out with Rob so they do not communicate with each other.

TERMS

Peter is _____ Rob at the moment.

6 The release of the prisoners should have happened this time last year.

DUE

The prisoners _____ twelve months ago.

7 The college's academic reputation motivated me to apply for a place.

SPEAKS

The academic _____, which is why I applied.

8 Mark admitted that he was the source of that story about Sarah.

OWNED

Mark _____ the rumour about Sarah.

9 Tina still has no fear at all when she takes on a defensive role in games.

UTTERLY

Tina remains _____ a defender.

10 People were concerned that what he had said was not valid.

CONCERNS

There were serious _____ some of his claims.

Answer sheet: Key word transformation Test No. [ ]

Name _____ Date _____

Write your answers in capital letters, using one box per letter.

1.
2.
3.
4.
5.
6.
7.
8.
9.
10.

Cambridge C2 Proficiency

Use of English

Part 4

Test 4

Cambridge C2 Proficiency Use of English
Part 4   Key word transformation   **Test 4**

For questions 1–10, complete the second sentence, using the word given, so that it has a similar meaning to the first sentence. Do not change the word provided and use between three and eight words in total. In the separate answer sheet, write your answers in capital letters, using one box per letter.

1. If you have any medical prescriptions, please indicate this on the form.

    MEDICATION

    Please list on the form _____ by your doctor.

2. For some reason, the company cannot retain its staff for very long.

    RATE

    I wonder why the _____ so low at the firm.

3. She really should have mentioned that she was a qualified accountant.

    NEGLECTED

    If only she _____ her accountancy qualifications.

4. I hadn't expected Max and Emma to be so hostile towards one other.

    SUCH

    Witnessing _____ Max and Emma was a surprise.

5 Kelly's colleagues were extremely irritated by her tactless behaviour.

LACK

It was Kelly's lack _____ of her colleagues' irritation.

6 I do not like it when people imply that it was wrong of me to take the job.

IMPLICATION

I resent _____ not have accepted the position.

7 We needed support as it was a vital project affecting so many people.

STAKE

There was too _____ do the project without any help.

8 Getting the polio vaccination at an early age protected me against the disease.

BEEN

Having _____ a child, I have never contracted it.

9 The outcome of the trial was extremely difficult to predict.

TOUCH

It was _____ the defendant would be found guilty.

10 The general perception of both Ali and Bob is that they are quite cautious.

GENERALLY

Neither Ali nor Bob _____ risk takers.

Answer sheet: Key word transformation   Test No. [ ]

Name _____   **Date** _____

Write your answers in capital letters, using one box per letter.

1.
2.
3.
4.
5.
6.
7.
8.
9.
10.

Cambridge C2 Proficiency

Use of English

Part 4

Test 5

Cambridge C2 Proficiency Use of English

Part 4   Key word transformation   Test 5

For questions 1–10, complete the second sentence, using the word given, so that it has a similar meaning to the first sentence. Do not change the word provided and use between three and eight words in total. In the separate answer sheet, write your answers in capital letters, using one box per letter.

1 At the moment, the club's main focus is the recruitment of a new team coach.

   PROCESS

   The club _____ a new coach for the team.

2 The audience applauded the performance enthusiastically.

   ROUND

   The performance won a huge _____ the audience.

3 Helen has a way of persuading people which means she always gets her own way.

   HERS

   When Helen speaks in _____, she is hard to refuse.

4 The product is completely different to what is being advertised online.

   RESEMBLANCE

   The advertisement _____ the actual product.

5 There should be something like a social club for youngsters in the local area.

LINES

We need something _____ a local youth club.

6 We have improved a lot when you remember our terrible first performance.

CAST

If you _____ debut, you'll see our progress.

7 I very nearly had a confrontation with Jon about the stolen money.

VERGE

I _____ Jon about the theft.

8 It was surprising to discover that Roy leaving caused such a fall in sales.

WHICH

I had not realised the _____ fallen since Roy's departure.

9 I strongly disagreed with my boss expecting me to do unpaid work.

EXCEPTION

What I _____ expected to work for free.

10 There is no way she forgot about Lee's party after being reminded so much.

SLIPPED

Lee's party _____ after all our reminders.

Answer sheet: Key word transformation Test No.

Name _____ Date _____

Write your answers in capital letters, using one box per letter.

1.
2.
3.
4.
5.
6.
7.
8.
9.
10.

Cambridge C2 Proficiency
Use of English

Part 4

Test 6

Cambridge C2 Proficiency Use of English

Part 4   Key word transformation   Test 6

For questions 1–10, complete the second sentence, using the word given, so that it has a similar meaning to the first sentence. Do not change the word provided and use between three and eight words in total. In the separate answer sheet, write your answers in capital letters, using one box per letter.

1. Many other local towns wish they had something like our new shopping centre.

   ENVY

   Our new shopping centre _____ entire region.

2. Sue did absolutely everything she could to help us.

   WAY

   Sue really _____ assistance to us.

3. Most politicians have no idea about what most people actually care about.

   TOUCH

   I think politicians _____ voters and their needs.

4. None of Ian's colleagues have a bad word to say about him.

   HIGHLY

   Ian _____ everyone he works with.

5 In most ways, Lou is now running things.

INTENTS

Lou is _____ charge now.

6 You will need to be very diplomatic when you tell him what has happened.

BREAK

You ought _____ him as carefully as possible.

7 I have never seen a vase with such a design before.

KIND

This vase truly _____ in design terms.

8 Nobody knew how to respond to David's emotional outburst.

LOST

Everyone _____ following David's speech.

9 As the main headquarters are closing soon, we will have to find a new base.

IMMINENT

Given _____ head office, we will be relocating.

10 Resources must no longer be allocated unfairly if we want to improve society.

FAIRER

The _____ for society to thrive.

Answer sheet: Key word transformation   Test No.

Name _____   Date _____

Write your answers in capital letters, using one box per letter.

1.

2.

3.

4.

5.

6.

7.

8.

9.

10.

Cambridge C2 Proficiency

Use of English

Part 4

Test 7

Cambridge C2 Proficiency Use of English
Part 4 — Key word transformation — Test 7

For questions 1–10, complete the second sentence, using the word given, so that it has a similar meaning to the first sentence. Do not change the word provided and use between three and eight words in total. In the separate answer sheet, write your answers in capital letters, using one box per letter.

1 You cannot tell for sure whether people behave differently in private.

   DOORS

   What _____ is not something we can ever know.

2 The property came to Alice as inheritance from a relative she barely knew.

   DISTANT

   Alice _____ relative.

3 Max having to work for Joe, his former employee, added irony to the situation.

   ASPECT

   The _____ Max used to be Joe's boss.

4 What helped us improve our performance was hearing our fans' cheers.

   SPURRED

   Our fans' vocal support _____ when we were getting tired.

5 The witnesses contradicted each other when describing the incident to the police.

ACCOUNTS

The witnesses _____ what had happened to the police.

6 Bill performed not quite as well as Sue in the interview.

EDGE

It was decided that _____ Bill in the interview.

7 His bad mood was because he had not had any sleep the previous night.

WINK

Having _____ whole night, he was very irritable.

8 They will have followed every single rule so that they can pass the inspection.

BOOK

Everything _____ to satisfy the inspectors.

9 Sadly, all the best parts of the original novel were lacking in the film version.

JUSTICE

The film adaptation _____ the original novel.

10 Mr Jones always finds the top qualities and talents that his students have.

BRING

Mr Jones always manages _____ his students.

Answer sheet: Key word transformation Test No. ☐

Name _____ **Date** _____

Write your answers in capital letters, using one box per letter.

1.
2.
3.
4.
5.
6.
7.
8.
9.
10.

Cambridge C2 Proficiency

Use of English

Part 4

Test 8

Cambridge C2 Proficiency Use of English

Part 4   Key word transformation   **Test 8**

For questions 1–10, complete the second sentence, using the word given, so that it has a similar meaning to the first sentence. Do not change the word provided and use between three and eight words in total. In the separate answer sheet, write your answers in capital letters, using one box per letter.

1. They have to forget their rivalries and focus instead on solving the problem.

   SIDE

   They must _____ if they want to fix the problem.

2. Small rooms appear larger than they actually are when they are full of light colours.

   ILLUSION

   Using light colours can _____ space in small rooms.

3. The worry is that we are no longer quite as dominant over other travel companies.

   DECLINING

   Our _____ sector is concerning.

4. The way the story ends is fairly ambiguous.

   AMOUNT

   The book leaves _____ in terms of the ending.

5 It's important to remember that not everyone is as fortunate as we are.

SPARE

Let's _____ less fortunate than ourselves.

6 If nobody else manages to fix the problem, I suppose we'll have to ask Ben.

LAST

We should _____ after trying other solutions first.

7 The council should have considered how the plan could potentially affect us.

STOCK

We wish the council _____ impacts of the plan.

8 Rob is not someone I would want to make angry in a professional setting.

BOOKS

I would hate _____ in the workplace.

9 I did not know how I felt about Ali backing me so publicly.

MAKE

I was not sure _____ that Ali had given me.

10 The negative press about the government is causing the erosion of people's trust.

BEING

The public's _____ by all the media scandals.

Answer sheet: Key word transformation Test No. ☐

Name _____ Date _____

Write your answers in capital letters, using one box per letter.

1.
2.
3.
4.
5.
6.
7.
8.
9.
10.

Cambridge C2 Proficiency
Use of English

Part 4

Test 9

Cambridge C2 Proficiency Use of English

Part 4 — Key word transformation — **Test 9**

For questions 1–10, complete the second sentence, using the word given, so that it has a similar meaning to the first sentence. Do not change the word provided and use between three and eight words in total. In the separate answer sheet, write your answers in capital letters, using one box per letter.

1. I do not have permission to tell you how the new policy will work.

   LIBERTY

   I _____ any details about the new policy.

2. To his credit, Ross really does know how to negotiate a deal.

   HAND

   You have _____ and his excellent negotiating skills.

3. Luckily, I found a shop with the comic I needed to complete my collection.

   STROKE

   It was _____ a shop selling what I had been looking for.

4. Sarah gets far more freedom than Jon, but she's just six months older.

   THAT

   Jon is still treated like a child, but he is _____ Sarah.

5 I will struggle to understand all the course content before the test.

GRIPS

It will be hard _____ everything before the exam.

6 I'd consider giving a presentation about your research results to the manager.

WHILE

It might _____ your findings to the manager.

7 Adam constantly begged Sarah to forgive him but she ignored his apologies.

PLEAS

Despite his _____, Sarah never spoke to Adam again.

8 I think oil companies are so hypocritical when they say that they care about nature.

SHEER

It is _____ they want to protect the environment.

9 We have only just begun to understand what artificial intelligence can do for business.

INFANCY

Artificial intelligence is _____ as a commercial prospect.

10 That minister has never made it clear whether he supports tax cuts.

STANDS

It is hard to know _____ the issue of taxation.

Answer sheet: Key word transformation Test No.

Name _____ **Date** _____

Write your answers in capital letters, using one box per letter.

1.
2.
3.
4.
5.
6.
7.
8.
9.
10.

Cambridge C2 Proficiency

Use of English

Part 4

Test 10

Cambridge C2 Proficiency Use of English
Part 4 — Key word transformation — Test 10

For questions 1–10, complete the second sentence, using the word given, so that it has a similar meaning to the first sentence. Do not change the word provided and use between three and eight words in total. In the separate answer sheet, write your answers in capital letters, using one box per letter.

1. The university has started building the new lecture theatre ahead of the new academic year.

   UNDER

   Construction of the lecture theatre _____ and will complete by September.

2. I don't even want to imagine Paula's reaction if she had been told the news.

   DREAD

   I _____ to the news.

3. I doubt the university even considered calling off the event.

   QUESTION

   Cancelling the event _____ for the university.

4. Keeping my main client is the most important thing to me.

   RUN

   I am not willing _____ my most important client.

5 Zoe's decision to drive in such terrible weather seemed like recklessness.

STRIKE

It did _____ Zoe to drive on such icy roads.

6 During the product launch, all eyes were on the marketing director.

CENTRE

The marketing director _____ at the product launch.

7 I cannot see how anyone can interpret the novel as being about politics.

POLITICAL

I feel that _____ are misguided.

8 Before we start, let's find out what builders are likely to charge for the work.

OBTAIN

We should _____ local builders before going ahead.

9 Since most people cannot afford to live in the city, they commute instead.

SCARCE

As _____ here, commuting is very common.

10 The officials never indicated that they were seeking a prosecution for shoplifting.

SLIGHTEST

Officials did not show even _____ the shoplifter.

Answer sheet: Key word transformation Test No. [ ]

Name _____ Date _____

Write your answers in capital letters, using one box per letter.

1.
2.
3.
4.
5.
6.
7.
8.
9.
10.

Cambridge C2 Proficiency

Use of English

Part 4

Test 11

Cambridge C2 Proficiency Use of English

Part 4 — Key word transformation — **Test 11**

For questions 1–10, complete the second sentence, using the word given, so that it has a similar meaning to the first sentence. Do not change the word provided and use between three and eight words in total. In the separate answer sheet, write your answers in capital letters, using one box per letter.

1. She had not studied at a famous university, but that didn't affect her job opportunities.

   HAVING

   She found a great job _____ from a top university.

2. Local campaigners are disgusted by the council's decision concerning public transport.

   MUCH

   The council is cutting bus services, _____ local campaigners.

3. I do not think I have ever been served by such a rude shop assistant before.

   RANK

   That _____ service I have ever experienced.

4. The speed with which your fitness declines after giving up exercise is surprising.

   SHAPE

   It is incredible _____ when you stop exercising.

5 Given how I was feeling at the time, I could not be Ali's representative.

FRAME

I was not in the _____ Ali.

6 She has enough musical talent not to have to rely on her famous family.

OWN

She is a talented musician _____, not just a pop star's daughter.

7 Nothing I do is ever good enough for my boss.

FAULT

My boss always manages _____ I do.

8 Decisions about wealth redistribution are made by government ministers.

DECIDE

It is government ministers _____ wealth across society.

9 My assistant has taken over for me so that I can focus on my recovery.

DUTIES

I have _____ while I recover from the operation.

10 Paula and Marcus could not differ more in terms of their ideas of fun.

POLES

Paula and Marcus _____ comes to their interests.

Answer sheet: Key word transformation Test No. ☐

Name _____ **Date** _____

Write your answers in capital letters, using one box per letter.

1.
2.
3.
4.
5.
6.
7.
8.
9.
10.

Cambridge C2 Proficiency

Use of English

Part 4

Test 12

Cambridge C2 Proficiency Use of English

Part 4   Key word transformation   Test 12

For questions 1–10, complete the second sentence, using the word given, so that it has a similar meaning to the first sentence. Do not change the word provided and use between three and eight words in total. In the separate answer sheet, write your answers in capital letters, using one box per letter.

1. Val's community work exemplifies what can be achieved at a local level.

   PRIME

   Val's community work _____ the power of local groups.

2. I think that fines deter people from parking illegally.

   SERVE

   Fines _____ people parking where they should not.

3. Lara wanted her sore throat to be taken into consideration during the audition.

   ALLOWANCES

   Lara hoped that the audition panel _____ sore throat.

4. She really wanted to be invited to your party.

   DAY

   It _____ to receive an invitation to your party.

5 My dad has achieved the awesome feat of running six marathons in a week.

AWE

I _____ achievements as a runner.

6 I wasn't able to identify what was making Sue seem different.

FINGER

Sue seemed different, but I could _____ had changed.

7 I think it's likely that being recommended by Stefan helped Helga get the role.

LIKELIHOOD

The reason Helga was hired _____ to Stefan's recommendation.

8 With all his web-design experience, Lee should be involved in the project.

HAVE

We should _____ project website.

9 I was relieved that the actor sensitively portrayed what it is like to grieve.

PORTRAYAL

The actor's _____, which I was pleased about.

10 The suspect's presence at the property is one conclusion we can draw, given the evidence.

MAY

From the evidence, it _____ at the house.

Answer sheet: Key word transformation Test No.

Name _____ Date _____

Write your answers in capital letters, using one box per letter.

1.
2.
3.
4.
5.
6.
7.
8.
9.
10.

Cambridge C2 Proficiency

Use of English

Part 4

Test 13

Cambridge C2 Proficiency Use of English

Part 4 — Key word transformation — **Test 13**

For questions 1–10, complete the second sentence, using the word given, so that it has a similar meaning to the first sentence. Do not change the word provided and use between three and eight words in total. In the separate answer sheet, write your answers in capital letters, using one box per letter.

1. When someone passes by the sensor, that should activate the security light automatically.

   MEANT

   The light _____ whenever the sensor detects movement.

2. We have to wait for official permission before we can issue statements to the media.

   PROCEED

   Please _____ until we have received permission.

3. Theatre adaptations are not really suitable for this particular novel.

   LEND

   The novel does not _____ for the stage.

4. Making hasty decisions might potentially lead us to overlook key evidence.

   JUMP

   Were _____, we could miss something vital.

5 I think that Kate seemed excessively angry about what was a minor mistake.

PROPORTION

Kate's anger _____ the size of the mistake.

6 I can only imagine the client's negative reaction had we not been on time.

KINDLY

The client _____ us arriving late.

7 I know the resignation was her decision, but it was still a shame.

ACCORD

She _____, but I wish she had stayed.

8 At the moment, we just cannot seem to win a single match.

PATCH

Our team is going _____ in terms of results.

9 Actors have to expect some negative criticism from time to time.

PARCEL

Receiving bad reviews _____ an actor.

10 I was so relieved when our puppy came home completely unharmed.

SOUND

Our puppy _____ a huge relief.

Answer sheet: Key word transformation　　　　Test No. ☐

Name _____　　**Date** _____

Write your answers in capital letters, using one box per letter.

1.

2.

3.

4.

5.

6.

7.

8.

9.

10.

Cambridge C2 Proficiency
Use of English

Part 4

Test 14

Cambridge C2 Proficiency Use of English

Part 4   Key word transformation   **Test 14**

For questions 1–10, complete the second sentence, using the word given, so that it has a similar meaning to the first sentence. Do not change the word provided and use between three and eight words in total. In the separate answer sheet, write your answers in capital letters, using one box per letter.

1. Do not underestimate how severe this situation is.

   APPRECIATE

   I do not think that you _____ this matter.

2. The economic situation is bound to improve soon.

   TAKE

   We are confident that the economy _____ before long.

3. Creating a negative depiction of Mary just for laughs is something I'd never do.

   DREAM

   I _____ negative light just to be humourous.

4. Don't worry if you need to miss the meeting because I'll be taking notes.

   END

   As I will be taking notes, it would _____ you were absent.

5 Given how dominant Isabel's team is, it will take us a while to establish ourselves.

DOMINANCE

We cannot expect instant success, what _____ Isabel's team.

6 As soon as things cease to be easy, Laura has a tendency to quit.

MINUTE

Lucy gives up _____ difficulty.

7 Feel free to give the kids a ring again if it stops you worrying about them.

PEACE

If it _____, you can call the kids again.

8 I'm sure her punishing workload did nothing to help her health.

TOLL

Working so hard must _____ physical health.

9 You should not have shared that information as it was strictly confidential.

STRICTEST

What I told you _____, and not something to be shared.

10 I'm glad the police intervened because it possibly stopped the situation from getting worse.

BEEN

If it had not _____, the situation might have escalated.

Answer sheet: Key word transformation Test No. ☐

Name _____ Date _____

Write your answers in capital letters, using one box per letter.

1.
2.
3.
4.
5.
6.
7.
8.
9.
10.

Cambridge C2 Proficiency Use of English

Part 4

Test 15

Cambridge C2 Proficiency Use of English

Part 4 Key word transformation Test 15

For questions 1–10, complete the second sentence, using the word given, so that it has a similar meaning to the first sentence. Do not change the word provided and use between three and eight words in total. In the separate answer sheet, write your answers in capital letters, using one box per letter.

1 I refused the role because I did not want to be posted to the New York office for two years.

   MEANT

   Accepting the role _____ the New York office for two years.

2 People thought that the council should not have commemorated such a controversial event.

   FIRE

   The council _____ such a controversial event.

3 This policy has the potential to cause employees to argue with each other.

   RISE

   The new proposal _____ between staff.

4 Having a cold meant that I couldn't appreciate the food at the party at all.

   WASTED

   Such good catering _____ me due to my cold.

5 We cannot ban vehicles unless public transport is improved at the same time.

CONJUNCTION

The ban will only work if it _____ public transport.

6 Flying to Spain was an impulsive idea rather than a trip we had planned.

SPUR

We decided to fly to Madrid _____ last weekend.

7 The neighbourhood desperately needed local amenities.

CRYING

The area _____ shops and leisure facilities.

8 Sebastian definitely will not be able to play in the match because of his injury.

RULED

Sebastian's injury means he has _____ the match.

9 Experts believe that, in general, the king showed mercy to his subjects.

RULER

He was thought _____ in most matters.

10 The necklace has been in our family for years.

HANDED

That necklace _____ one generation to the next for years.

Answer sheet: Key word transformation Test No.

Name _____ Date _____

Write your answers in capital letters, using one box per letter.

Cambridge C2 Proficiency

Use of English

Part 4

Test 16

Cambridge C2 Proficiency Use of English

Part 4 Key word transformation Test 16

For questions 1–10, complete the second sentence, using the word given, so that it has a similar meaning to the first sentence. Do not change the word provided and use between three and eight words in total. In the separate answer sheet, write your answers in capital letters, using one box per letter.

1 Party members are extremely divided on how best to help homeless people.

   TEARING

   It is the issue of _____ the party.

2 As Tomas is Julia's brother, she will obviously support him to protect him from criticism.

   STICK

   Julia is certain _____ of family loyalty.

3 Louise's offence at the vulgarity of the joke was visible to everyone in the room.

   OFFENDED

   Louise _____ such a vulgar joke.

4 Withdrawal is inevitable if we cannot meet all the tournament expenses.

   PROSPECT

   Unless we raise enough funds, we _____ from the tournament.

5 It was quite an achievement to set a new race record while there was torrential rain.

MEAN

Setting a new record was _____ adverse weather conditions.

6 Your final grade will not include the class-presentation mark.

COUNT

Your presentation score _____ your final grade.

7 The authorities seem to be dealing with minor crimes more severely now.

CRACKING

The authorities are showing signs _____ petty crime.

8 Sarah's main strength lies in technology rather than being able to persuade.

STRONG

Sarah's powers of _____ IT skills.

9 Lisa found it hard to stop herself from laughing as she lied to the teacher.

STRAIGHT

Lisa could barely _____ lying to her teacher.

10 When I heard the man speak, I'll never forget how desperate he seemed.

DESPERATION

What I remember about the man was the _____ he spoke.

Answer sheet: Key word transformation Test No.

Name _____ **Date** _____

Write your answers in capital letters, using one box per letter.

1.

2.

3.

4.

5.

6.

7.

8.

9.

10.

Cambridge C2 Proficiency

Use of English

Part 4

Test 17

Cambridge C2 Proficiency Use of English
Part 4 — Key word transformation — Test 17

For questions 1–10, complete the second sentence, using the word given, so that it has a similar meaning to the first sentence. Do not change the word provided and use between three and eight words in total. In the separate answer sheet, write your answers in capital letters, using one box per letter.

1 Most of the noise from the street was reduced when they got double-glazed windows.

   BARELY

   After better windows were fitted, _____ heard from outside.

2 My house is just as messy as it was last week.

   START

   I still haven't _____ the house yet.

3 If local environmental groups oppose our plan, we should find an alternative.

   RUN

   Were we _____ from environmentalists, we would have to rethink our strategy.

4 Jake was sent off during the final, but Joe never held it against his teammate.

   RESENTMENT

   Joe _____ such an important mistake.

5 I took on a part-time job purely because I wanted to save up for my studies.

MEANS

Working part-time _____ to help me pay for university.

6 It was hard to tell the difference between the real document and the one that was forged.

REALISTIC

It was _____ of the actual document.

7 Removing freedom of speech defies the constitution of the country.

TAKE

It is simply _____ people's freedom of speech.

8 Sooner or later, you will start to be affected by your lifestyle choices.

CATCH

Your late nights and poor diet _____ you eventually.

9 It must be stressed that Lucas does the accounts extremely thoroughly.

NOTHING

Lucas is _____ as an accountant.

10 The fact that Gloria has a disability is irrelevant to her effectiveness as a manager.

BESIDE

Gloria's disability _____ when it comes to her work.

Answer sheet: Key word transformation Test No.

Name _____ Date _____

Write your answers in capital letters, using one box per letter.

1.
2.
3.
4.
5.
6.
7.
8.
9.
10.

Cambridge C2 Proficiency

Use of English

Part 4

Test 18

Cambridge C2 Proficiency Use of English

Part 4 — Key word transformation — **Test 18**

For questions 1–10, complete the second sentence, using the word given, so that it has a similar meaning to the first sentence. Do not change the word provided and use between three and eight words in total. In the separate answer sheet, write your answers in capital letters, using one box per letter.

1 Clearly, the minister has not officially announced his intention to resign.

   PUBLIC

   The minister's resignation can't have _____ yet.

2 Keeping a full-time job while taking care of my elderly parents is a challenge.

   HOLD

   It is not _____ my caring responsibilities.

3 I don't understand why she didn't complain to officials about being disqualified.

   APPEALED

   She ought _____ the competition.

4 Giving you advanced warning about their visit would have been considerate.

   INFORM

   It was very _____ their visit.

5 The assignments I am asked to work on are frustratingly simple.

ASSIGN

I wish my manager _____ cases.

6 Hardly anyone can afford to buy a house in that part of town.

REACH

Properties in that area are _____ most people.

7 We'll ensure that our meeting is not at the same time as their event.

CLASH

Should their event _____, we will reschedule.

8 He never wants to compromise, which is why we are getting concerned.

CAUSE

What is becoming _____ his refusal to compromise.

9 After some time, she began to regret her actions.

REMORSE

She eventually _____ she had done.

10 The punishment for his fraudulent insurance claims is about to be decided.

COMMITTING

He is due to be _____ shortly.

Answer sheet: Key word transformation Test No.

Name _____ Date _____

Write your answers in capital letters, using one box per letter.

1.
2.
3.
4.
5.
6.
7.
8.
9.
10.

Cambridge C2 Proficiency

Use of English

Part 4

Test 19

Cambridge C2 Proficiency Use of English

Part 4   Key word transformation   Test 19

For questions 1–10, complete the second sentence, using the word given, so that it has a similar meaning to the first sentence. Do not change the word provided and use between three and eight words in total. In the separate answer sheet, write your answers in capital letters, using one box per letter.

1. At that time, we could not afford to make any investment in the company.

   MEANS

   We simply did not _____ in the business.

2. She ensured that every single dollar of her wedding budget was spent wisely.

   SQUANDER

   Not a _____ unnecessary items for the wedding.

3. Experts believe that the water in the lake is too salty for fish to survive in it.

   CONCENTRATION

   The lack of fish is attributed _____ in the lake.

4. He would not even consider compromising with the staff on strike.

   WILLING

   He was not at _____ concessions to end the strike.

5 I don't know how she ignored all the attempts to provoke her.

RESPOND

She somehow managed _____ that came her way.

6 She noted that his attitude towards the execution of the plan seemed very upbeat.

OPTIMISM

She detected his _____ the plan.

7 Anna felt that her charity work was being overlooked by the media.

GREATER

Anna yearned _____ the media for her charity work.

8 Based on what I've heard so far, the idea could generate a lot of money.

SOUND

From _____, this idea could be very profitable.

9 I initially let my children be filmed for the documentary.

CONSENTED

At first, I _____ in the documentary.

10 It became increasingly hard to ignore all the terrible things that might happen.

FEAR

I tried my best _____ despite my growing concern.

Answer sheet: Key word transformation Test No. ☐

Name _____   Date _____

Write your answers in capital letters, using one box per letter.

1.

2.

3.

4.

5.

6.

7.

8.

9.

10.

Cambridge C2 Proficiency

Use of English

Part 4

Test 20

Cambridge C2 Proficiency Use of English

Part 4   Key word transformation   **Test 20**

For questions 1–10, complete the second sentence, using the word given, so that it has a similar meaning to the first sentence. Do not change the word provided and use between three and eight words in total. In the separate answer sheet, write your answers in capital letters, using one box per letter.

1 There wasn't a moment when I wasn't feeling nervous about the interview.

   EDGE

   I _____ day thinking about the interview.

2 I think not having IT knowledge held me back when I was looking for a job.

   DISADVANTAGE

   My poor IT skills probably _____ in the job market.

3 We'd love to work with you again as long as the client is happy with this project.

   SATISFACTION

   If you do the work _____ client, we'll hire you again.

4 His enthusiasm made it hard for me to make sense of his ideas.

   TRAIN

   I struggled _____ as he was so animated.

5 Above all, the campaign would encourage people to use renewable energy.

PRIMARILY

The campaign _____ the use of fossil fuels.

6 I'm not trying to get you to change your goals in life.

PURSUING

It is not my intention to talk _____ your dream.

7 I have no idea why people behaved so irrationally during the conference.

ACCOUNT

I wonder what _____ at the conference.

8 Sadly, my shyness stopped me from seeing if she wanted to date me.

PLUCKED

I wish I had _____ on a date before it was too late.

9 The media simply does not have the right to know about my private life.

INVASION

I will not tolerate _____ by the media.

10 It strikes me that the company understands its customers' needs and interests.

TUNE

The company always seems _____ customers expect.

Answer sheet: Key word transformation Test No. ☐

Name _____ **Date** _____

Write your answers in capital letters, using one box per letter.

1. ☐☐☐☐☐☐☐☐☐☐☐☐☐☐☐
2. ☐☐☐☐☐☐☐☐☐☐☐☐☐☐☐
3. ☐☐☐☐☐☐☐☐☐☐☐☐☐☐☐
4. ☐☐☐☐☐☐☐☐☐☐☐☐☐☐☐
5. ☐☐☐☐☐☐☐☐☐☐☐☐☐☐☐
6. ☐☐☐☐☐☐☐☐☐☐☐☐☐☐☐
7. ☐☐☐☐☐☐☐☐☐☐☐☐☐☐☐
8. ☐☐☐☐☐☐☐☐☐☐☐☐☐☐☐
9. ☐☐☐☐☐☐☐☐☐☐☐☐☐☐☐
10. ☐☐☐☐☐☐☐☐☐☐☐☐☐☐☐

Answers

Answers — Cambridge C2 Proficiency Use of English — Test 1

1	was / came as	something of a surprise	L	G
2	pay Rob/him	(many/several) compliments (about his work)	G	L
3	failed to see/understand	the relevance/significance of	G	L
4	read	between the lines	G	L
5	were	to be passed	G	L
6	her/Pat	the benefit of the doubt	G	L
7	not to jump	to (any) conclusions	G	L
8	has/is yet	to convince voters that the policy	G	L
9	alleged	was too serious to	L	G
10	are in	the same boat as	G	L

Answers — Cambridge C2 Proficiency Use of English — Test 2

1	a/the gap	in the market for	G	L
2	long to	broaden/widen my	G	L
3	were not/weren't deemed	to be	L	G
4	single colleague / single one of her colleagues	had/showed (any)	G	L
5	effective route	to (achieving)	L	G
6	subjected the minster to	a range/lot/series	G	L
7	would sooner work	from/at	L	G
8	has/possesses	a wealth of (IT) knowledge / a wealth of knowledge about IT	G	L
9	she had put	her foot down with	G	L
10	was Louise who	coined the term/phrase	G	L

Answers — Cambridge C2 Proficiency Use of English — Test 3

1	is prone to	sulk / sulking / having a sulk	L	G
2	keep you	on your	L	G
3	only so many times	(that) we can	L	G
4	they were/kept	(constantly/always) complaining about	G	L
5	not on	speaking/good/friendly terms with	G	L
6	were due to be / were due to have been	released	G	L
7	reputation of the college	speaks for itself	G	L
8	owned up	to starting / to making up	L	G
9	remains	utterly fearless as	G	L
10	concerns (raised)	about (the validity of)	G	L

Answers — Cambridge C2 Proficiency Use of English — Test 4

1	any medication	prescribed / which/that has been prescribed	L	G
2	staff retention rate	is / seems to be	L	G
3	had not/hadn't neglected	to mention	G	L
4	such hostility	between	L	G
5	lack of tact	that was the cause/source	L	G
6	the implication that	I should	L	G
7	much	at stake to	G	L
8	been vaccinated	against polio as	G	L
9	touch and go	whether	L	G
10	are generally perceived / thought / considered	to be	L	G

Answers — Cambridge C2 Proficiency Use of English — Test 5

1	is in the process of	recruiting	G	L
2	round of applause	from	L	G
3	that persuasive way	of hers	L	G
4	bears/has	little/no resemblance to	G	L
5	along the lines	of	L	G
6	cast your mind back	to the/our	L	G
7	was on the verge of	confronting	G	L
8	extent to	which sales had	L	G
9	took exception to	was being	L	G
10	could not/couldn't have	slipped her mind	G	L

Answers — Cambridge C2 Proficiency Use of English — Test 6

1	is the envy	of the	L	G
2	went out of her way to	provide/offer / be of	G	L
3	are (completely)	out of touch with	G	L
4	is thought highly / is highly thought	of by	L	G
5	to	all intents and purposes in	G	L
6	to break	the news to	G	L
7	is	one of a kind	G	L
8	was	(completely) lost for words	G	L
9	the imminent closure	of the	L	G
10	allocation of resources	must be fairer / has/should/ought to be fairer	L	G

Answers — Cambridge C2 Proficiency Use of English — Test 7

1	goes on / happens / people do	behind closed doors	G	L
2	inherited the property	from a distant	L	G
3	ironic aspect of the situation	was/is that	L	G
4	spurred	us on (to play/perform better)	G	L
5	gave contradictory/different/conflicting	accounts of/about	L	G
6	Sue had the edge	on/over	L	G
7	not slept a wink / not had a wink of sleep	the	L	G
8	will have been done	by the book	G	L
9	did not/didn't do	justice to	G	L
10	to bring out	the best in	G	L

Answers — Cambridge C2 Proficiency Use of English — Test 8

1	put their differences/rivalries	to one side	L	G
2	create/give	an/the illusion of	G	L
3	declining dominance	in the tourism	G	L
4	a certain/fair amount of	ambiguity	G	L
5	spare a thought for	those/people (who are)	L	G
6	call/ask/contact Ben	as a last resort	G	L
7	had taken	stock of the potential	G	L
8	to be/get	in his/Rob's bad books	G	L
9	what to make	of the (public) backing	G	L
10	trust in the government	is being eroded	L	G

Answers — Cambridge C2 Proficiency Use of English — Test 9

1	am not at liberty to	share / reveal/disclose/announce / give you	G	L
2	have to hand	it to Ross	G	L
3	a stroke of luck	to have found / that I found	L	G
4	not that much	younger than	G	L
5	(for me) to get	to grips with	L	G
6	be worth your while	to present	L	G
7	(constant) pleas for	forgiveness	L	G
8	sheer hypocrisy for	oil companies to claim (that)	L	G
9	(still) in its	infancy	G	L
10	where he / where the minister	stands on	G	L

Answers — Cambridge C2 Proficiency Use of English — Test 10

1	is (already)	under way	L	G
2	dread to think	how she/Paula would have reacted	L	G
3	would have been	out of the question	G	L
4	to run the risk	of losing	L	G
5	strike me as	reckless of	G	L
6	was the	centre of attention	G	L
7	political interpretations	of the novel	L	G
8	obtain (some)	quotes/estimates from	G	L
9	affordable accommodation/housing is / affordable homes/properties are / affordable places to live are	scarce	G	L
10	the slightest intention of / the slightest interest in	prosecuting/charging	G	L

Answers — Cambridge C2 Proficiency Use of English — Test 11

1	despite not having / without having	graduated / a degree	G	L
2	much to the	disgust of	G	L
3	must rank as	the worst/rudest/most appalling (customer)	L	G
4	how fast/quickly/soon	you (can) get out of shape	G	L
5	right frame of mind	to represent	L	G
6	in	her own right	G	L
7	to find	fault with whatever/everything/anything	G	L
8	who decide how to	redistribute	G	L
9	been relieved of	my duties	G	L
10	are	poles apart when it	G	L

Answers — Cambridge C2 Proficiency Use of English — Test 12

1	is	a prime example of	G	L
2	serve as	deterrents to / a deterrent to	G	L
3	would make	allowances for her	G	L
4	would have made	her day	G	L
5	am	in awe of his / in awe of (my) dad's	G	L
6	not put	my finger on what had	G	L
7	was	in all likelihood due/thanks	G	L
8	have Lee/him	design our/the	G	L
9	portrayal of grief	was (extremely) sensitive	L	G
10	may be concluded	that the suspect had been	G	L

Answers — Cambridge C2 Proficiency Use of English — Test 13

1	is meant to	activate / be activated	G	L
2	do not proceed to	issue a statement / issue any statements	G	L
3	lend itself to	being adapted for / adaptation(s)	L	G
4	we to	jump to conclusions	G	L
5	was/seemed	out of proportion to	G	L
6	would not/wouldn't have	taken kindly to	G	L
7	quit/resigned/left	of her own accord	L	G
8	through a	bad/difficult/rough patch	G	L
9	is part and parcel	of being / of working as	L	G
10	returning (home) / coming back/home	safe and sound was	G	L

Answers — Cambridge C2 Proficiency Use of English — Test 14

1	appreciate	the severity of	L	G
2	will take	a turn for the better	G	L
3	would not/wouldn't dream of / would never dream of	depicting Mary in a	G	L
4	bot be	the end of the world if	G	L
5	with	the dominance of	G	L
6	the minute she / the minute that she / the minute	runs into / faces / encounters / there is	G	L
7	gives you	peace (of mind)	G	L
8	have taken	its toll on her	G	L
9	was in	the strictest confidence	G	L
10	been for	the police intervention/intervening / the intervention of the police	G	L

Answers — Cambridge C2 Proficiency Use of English — Test 15

1	would have meant	being posted to / having to work at / moving to / working at/in	G	L
2	came under fire for	commemorating/marking	G	L
3	may/could/might give	rise to disputes/arguments/conflicts	G	L
4	was	(completely) wasted on	G	L
5	is / is done / is implemented	in conjunction with better/improved / in conjunction with improvements to/in	G	L
6	on the	spur of the moment	G	L
7	was crying	out for (better/more/some)	G	L
8	to be ruled	out of / out of playing in	G	L
9	to be	a merciful ruler / a ruler that/who showed mercy	G	L
10	has been handed	down from	G	L

Answers — Cambridge C2 Proficiency Use of English — Test 16

1	homelessness	that/which is tearing apart	L	G
2	to stick up	for Tomas/him out/because	G	L
3	was visibly/clearly	offended by	G	L
4	will face / face	the prospect of withdrawing	G	L
5	no mean feat	in the/such/those / given the/such/those	L	G
6	will not/won't	count toward(s)	G	L
7	of cracking	down on	G	L
8	persuasion/persuading	are not/ aren't as strong as her	L	G
9	keep	a straight face when/while	G	L
10	(sense of) desperation	with which he / when/as he	L	G

Answers   Cambridge C2 Proficiency Use of English   Test 17

1	barely a sound / barely any noise	could be	L	G
2	made a start	on tidying/clearing/cleaning	G	L
3	to run	into/up against opposition	G	L
4	never had/showed (any)	resentment towards Jake for (making)	G	L
5	was (purely/simply/just) a	means to an end	G	L
6	was a (very)	realistic forgery/copy	G	L
7	not constitutional / unconstitutional	to take away	L	G
8	will catch	up with	G	L
9	nothing if not / nothing but	thorough	L	G
10	is	beside the point	G	L

Answers   Cambridge C2 Proficiency Use of English   Test 18

1	been made	public	G	L
2	(so) easy to	hold down a job alongside/during	G	L
3	to have appealed	against her/the disqualification from / against being disqualified from	G	L
4	inconsiderate/rude/thoughtless (of them)	not to inform you of	L	G
5	would assign (me)	more complex/challenging / less simple	G	L
6	beyond/out of the	(financial) reach of	G	L
7	clash with	our meeting	L	G
8	a cause	for concern is	L	G
9	felt/showed/experienced remorse	for what	L	G
10	sentenced/punished for committing	(insurance) fraud	G	L

Answers   Cambridge C2 Proficiency Use of English   Test 19

1	have the (financial) means	to invest	L	G
2	(single) dollar did she	squander on	G	L
3	to the (high) concentration	of salt	G	L
4	all willing	to make	L	G
5	not to respond to	(any/the) provocation / all the provocation	G	L
6	(sense of) optimism	about executing/carrying out	L	G
7	to get / for	greater recognition in/by / greater acknowledgment by	G	L
8	the sound of	it	L	G
9	consented to my children	appearing/featuring/being	G	L
10	not to fear	the worst	G	L

Answers   Cambridge C2 Proficiency Use of English   Test 20

1	was/felt on edge	the whole/entire / all	L	G
2	put/placed me	at a disadvantage	L	G
3	to the	satisfaction of the	G	L
4	to follow/understand / to keep up with	his train of thought	G	L
5	(would) primarily	discourage(d) / warn(ed) against	G	L
6	you out	of pursuing	G	L
7	could/would account for	such/the irrational behaviour	G	L
8	plucked up the courage	to ask her (out)	L	G
9	(such) an/any invasion(s) of	(my) privacy	G	L
10	(to be) in tune with	what (its)	L	G

Notes

Notes

Notes

www.ingramcontent.com/pod-product-compliance
Lightning Source LLC
Chambersburg PA
CBHW081918090526
44590CB00019B/3402